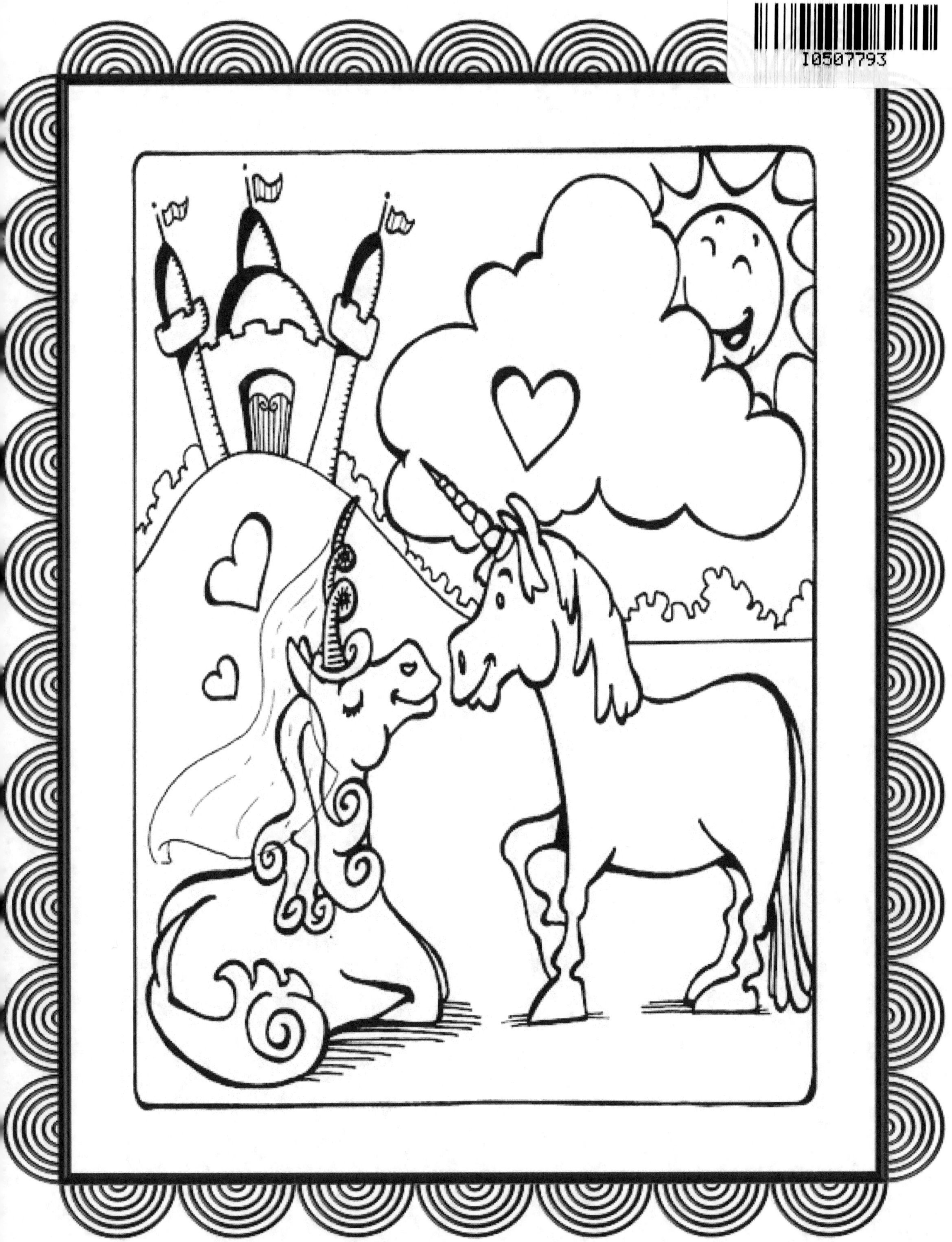

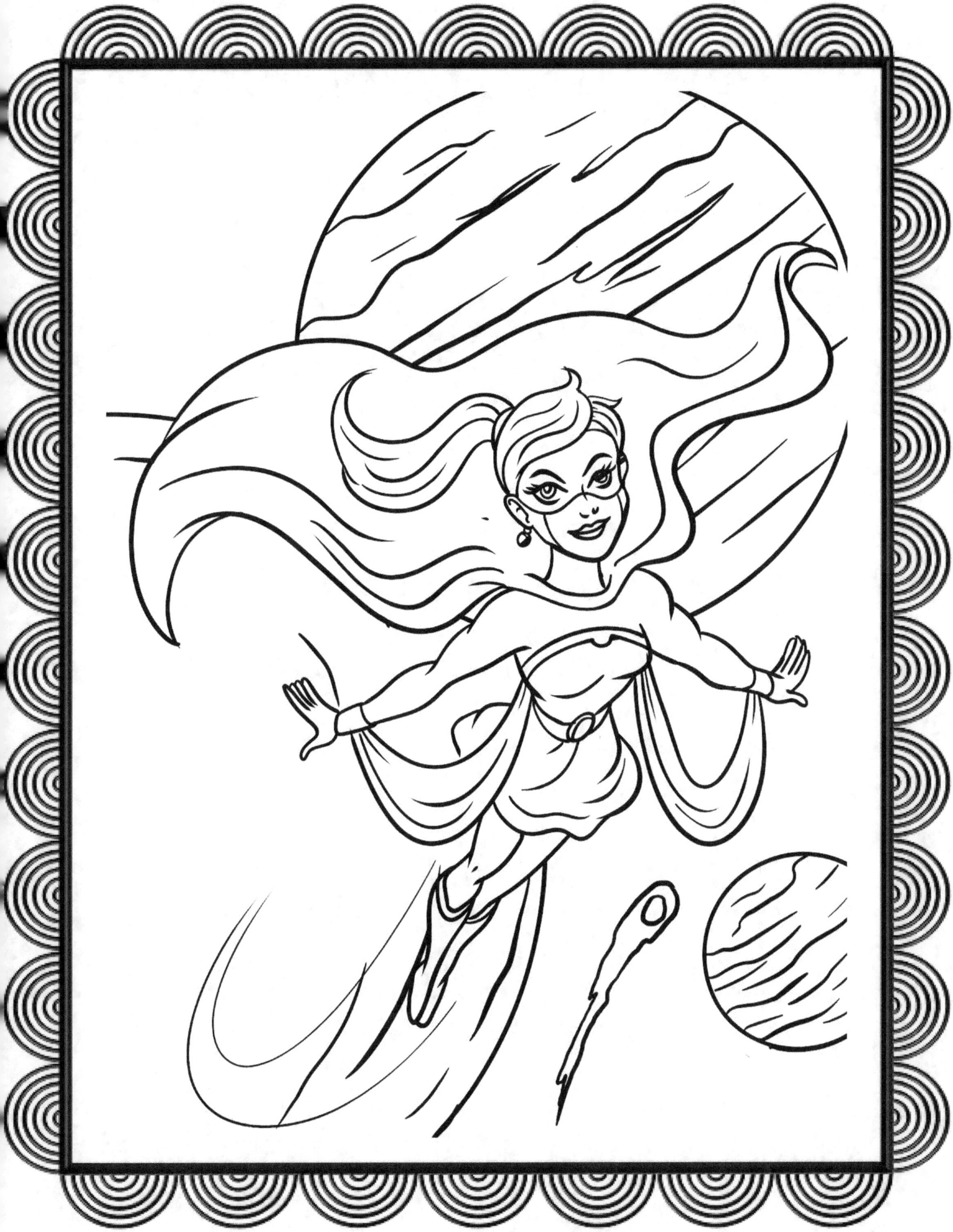

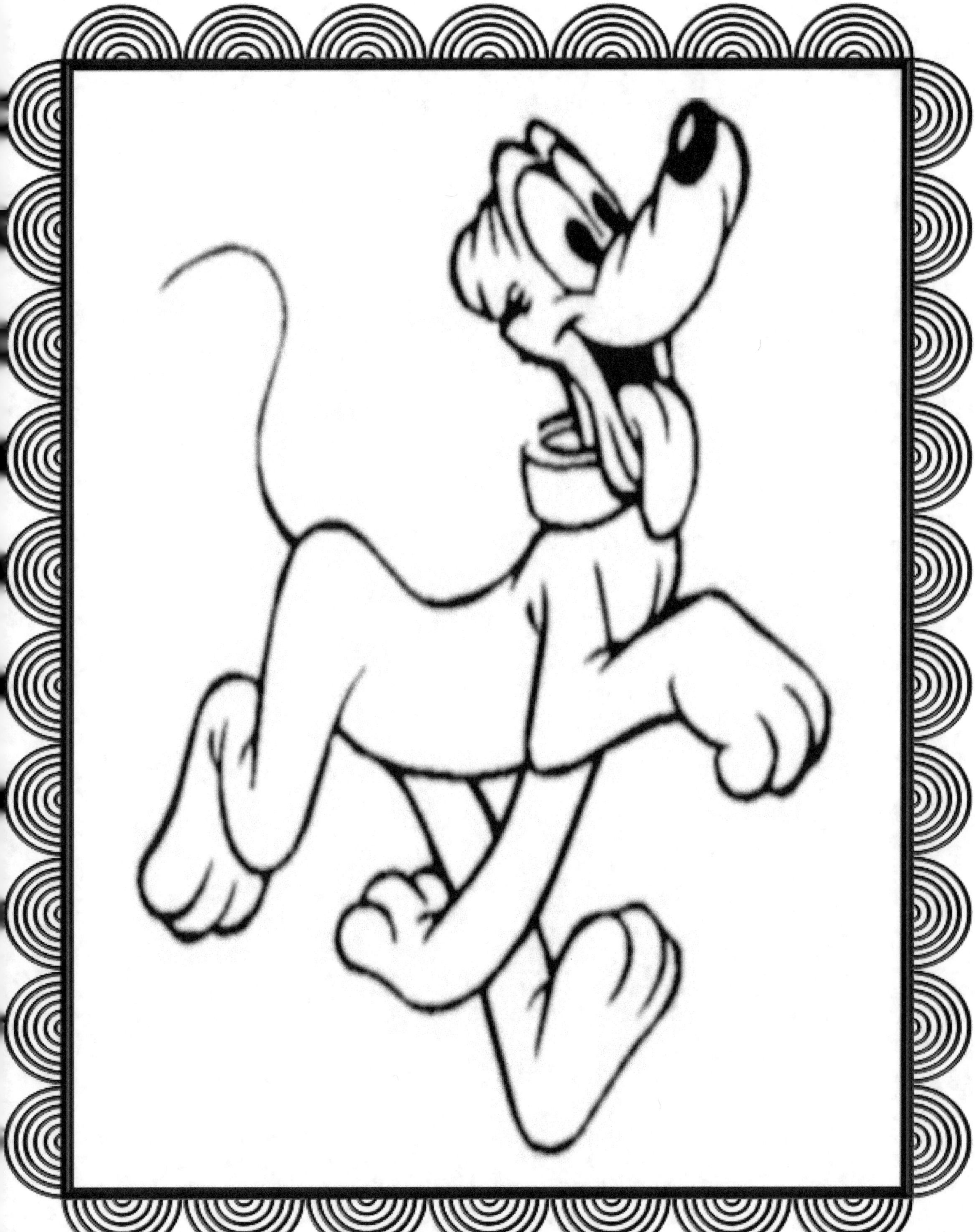

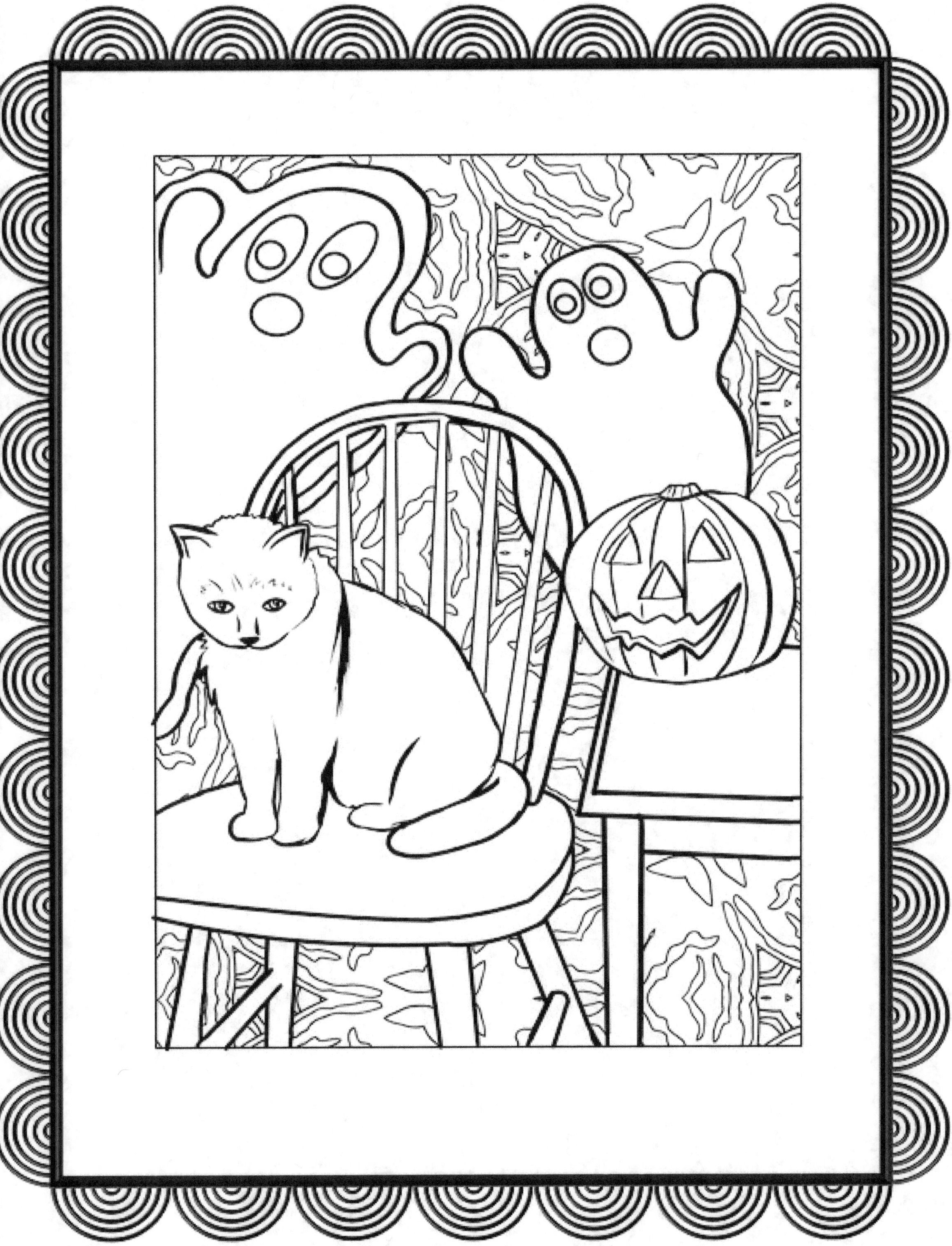

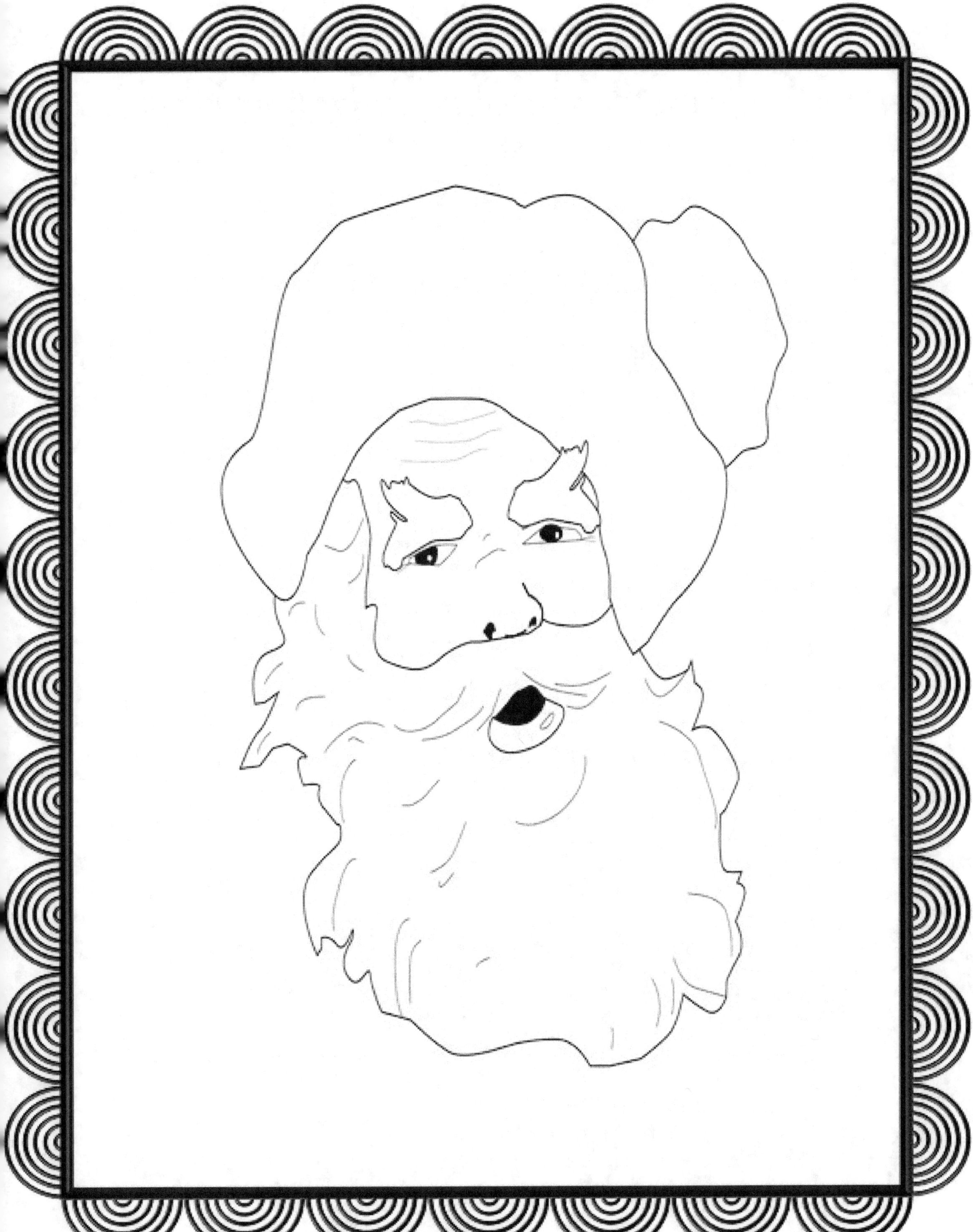

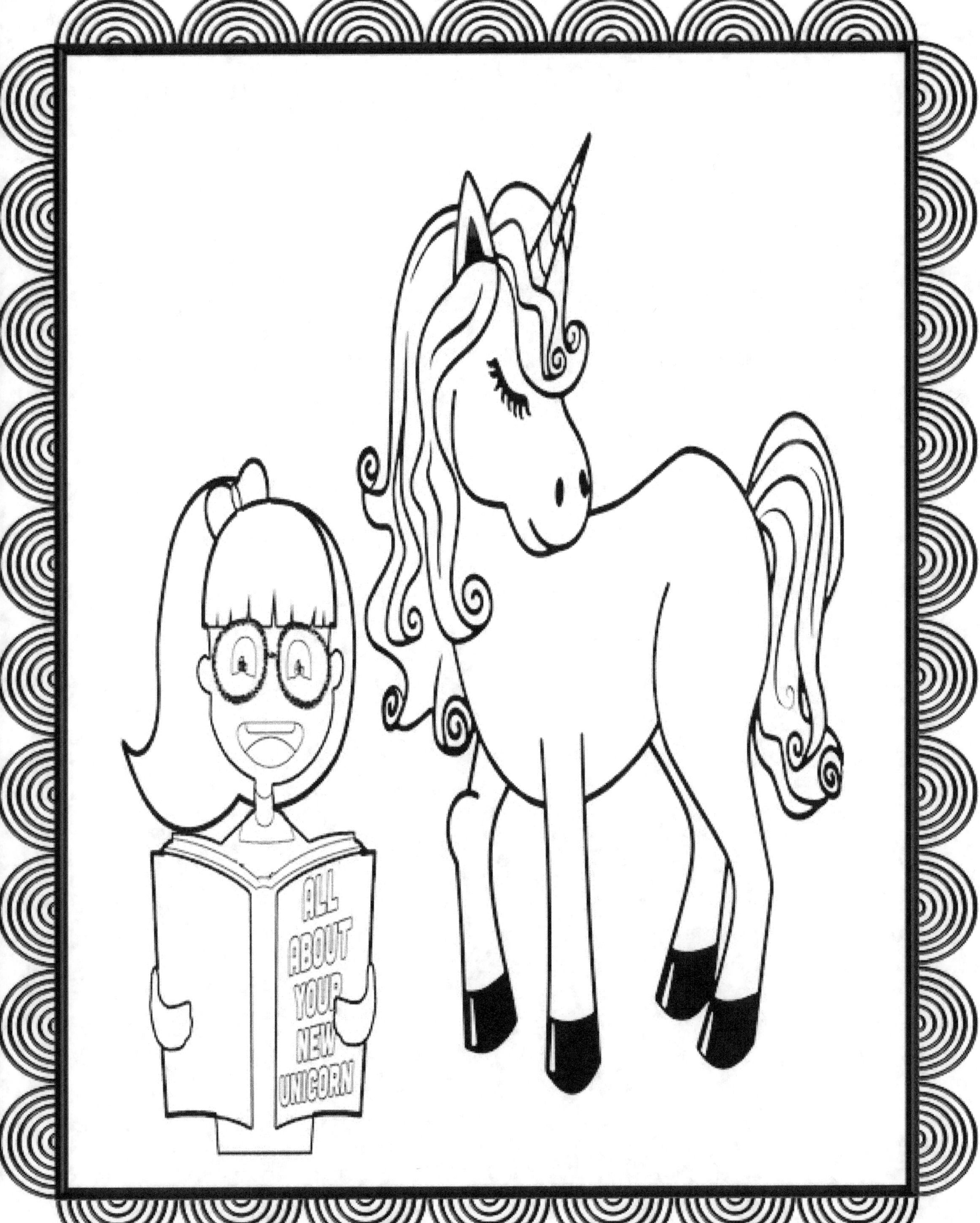
ALL ABOUT YOUR NEW UNICORN

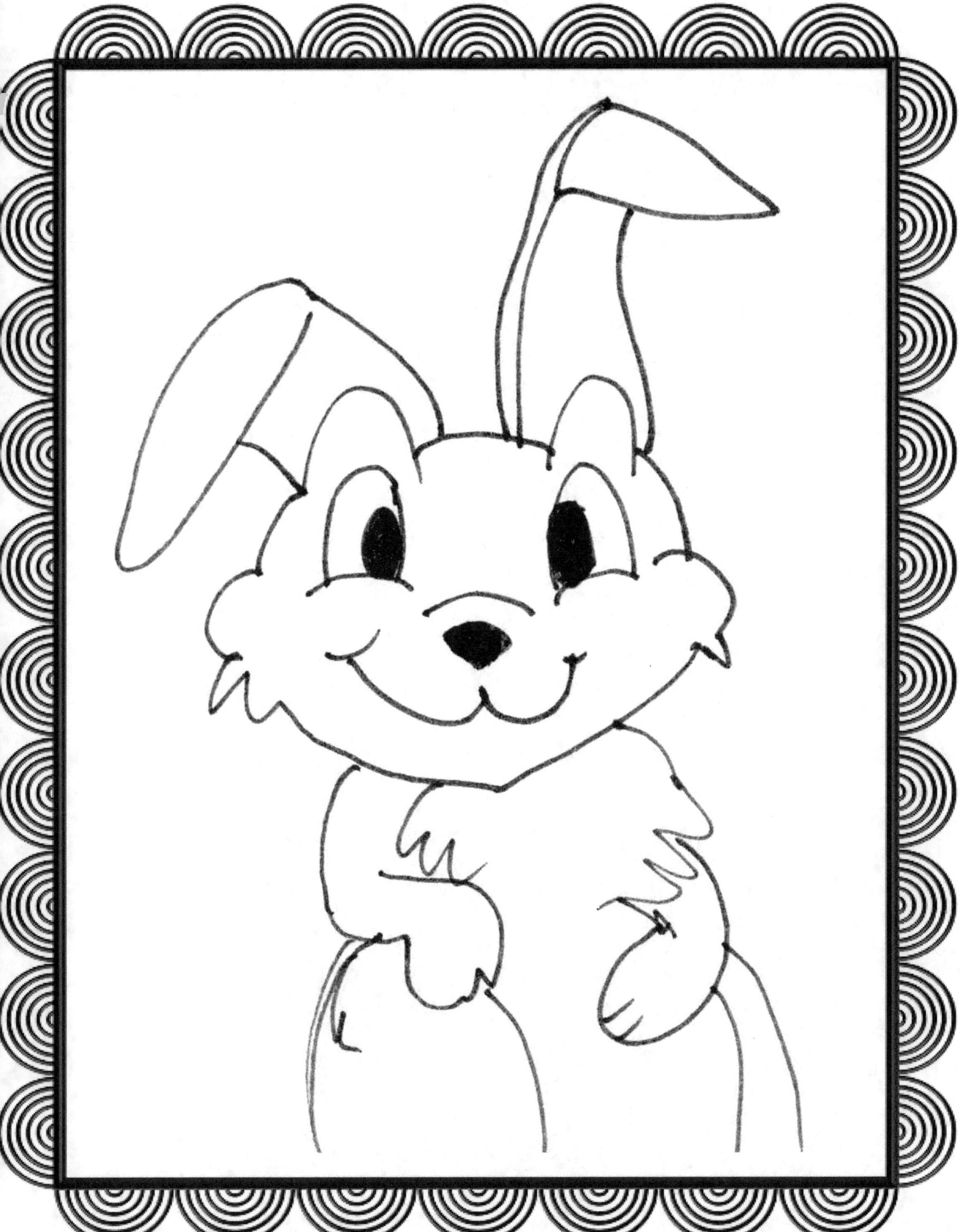

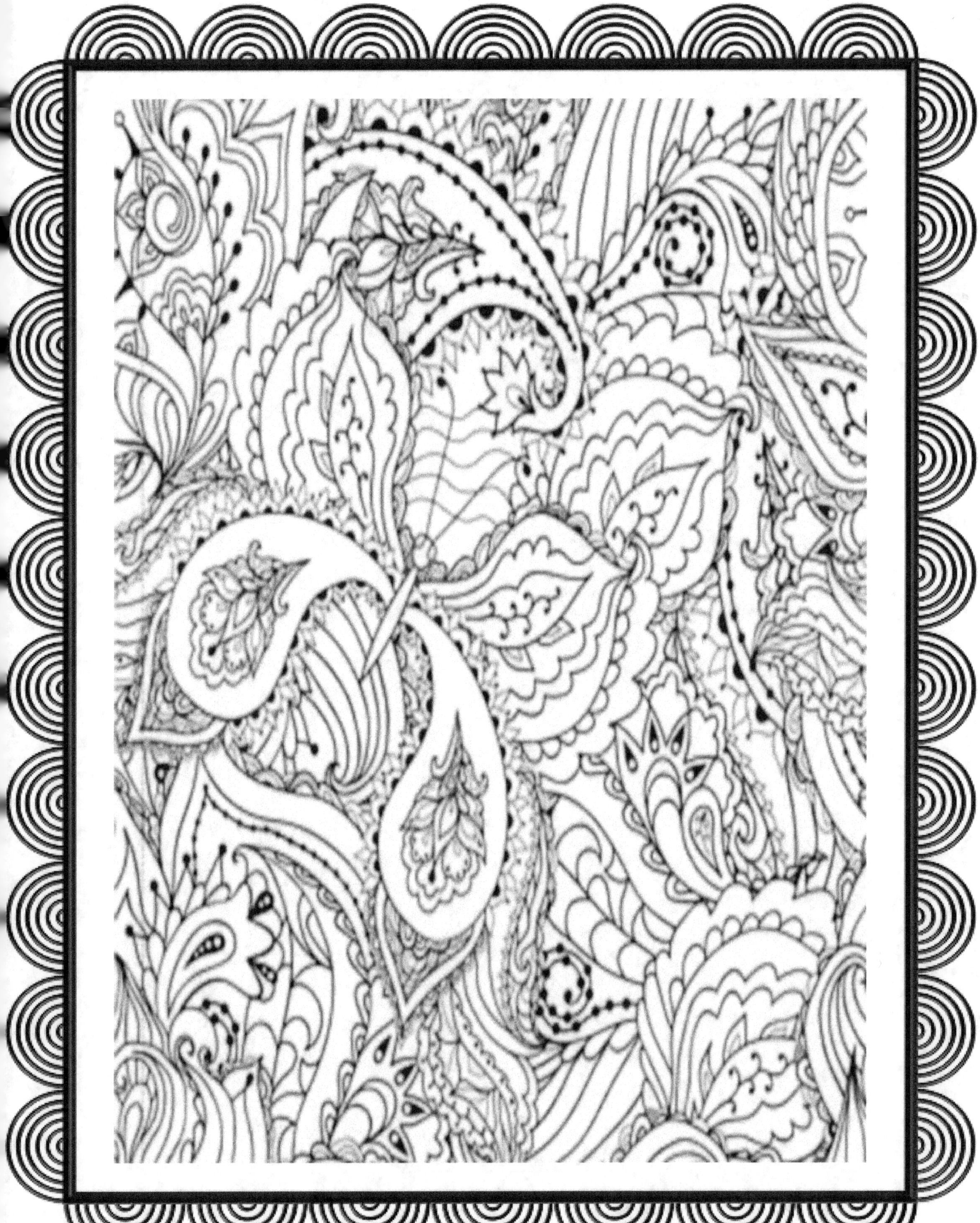

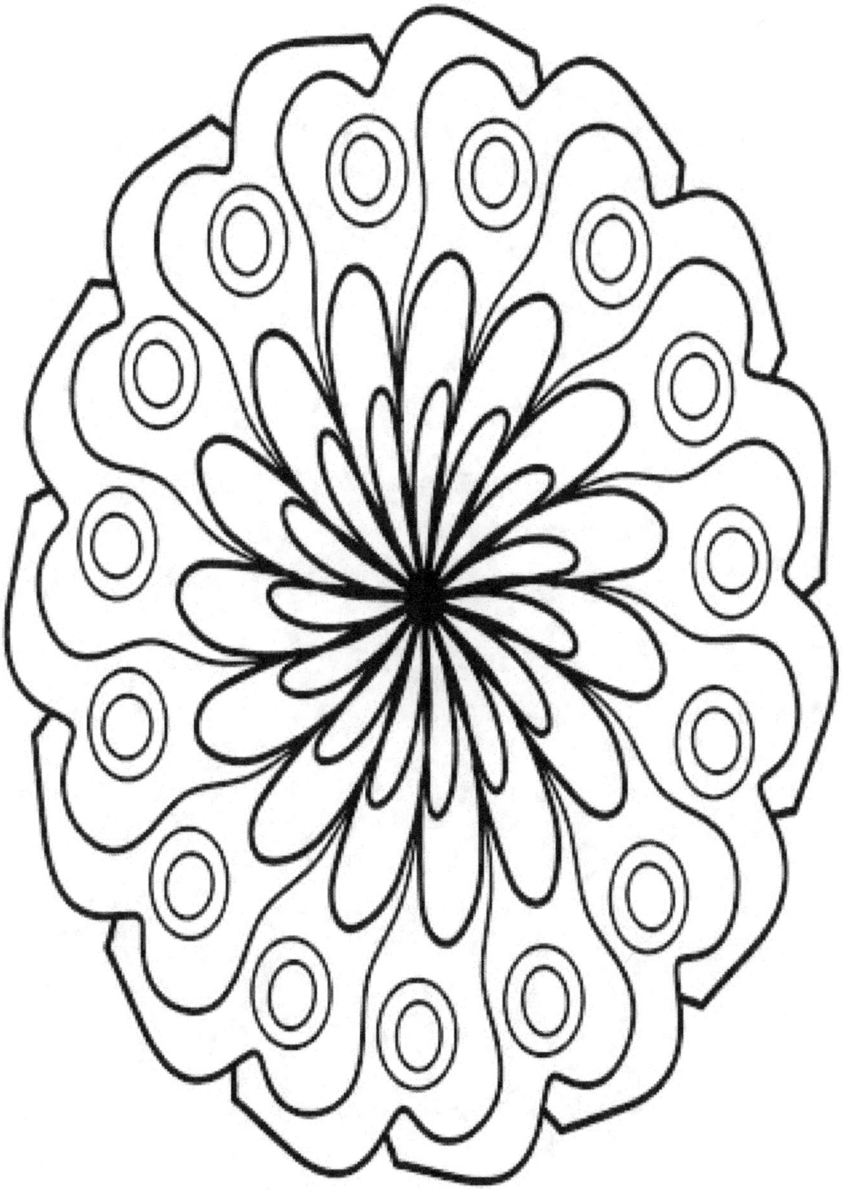

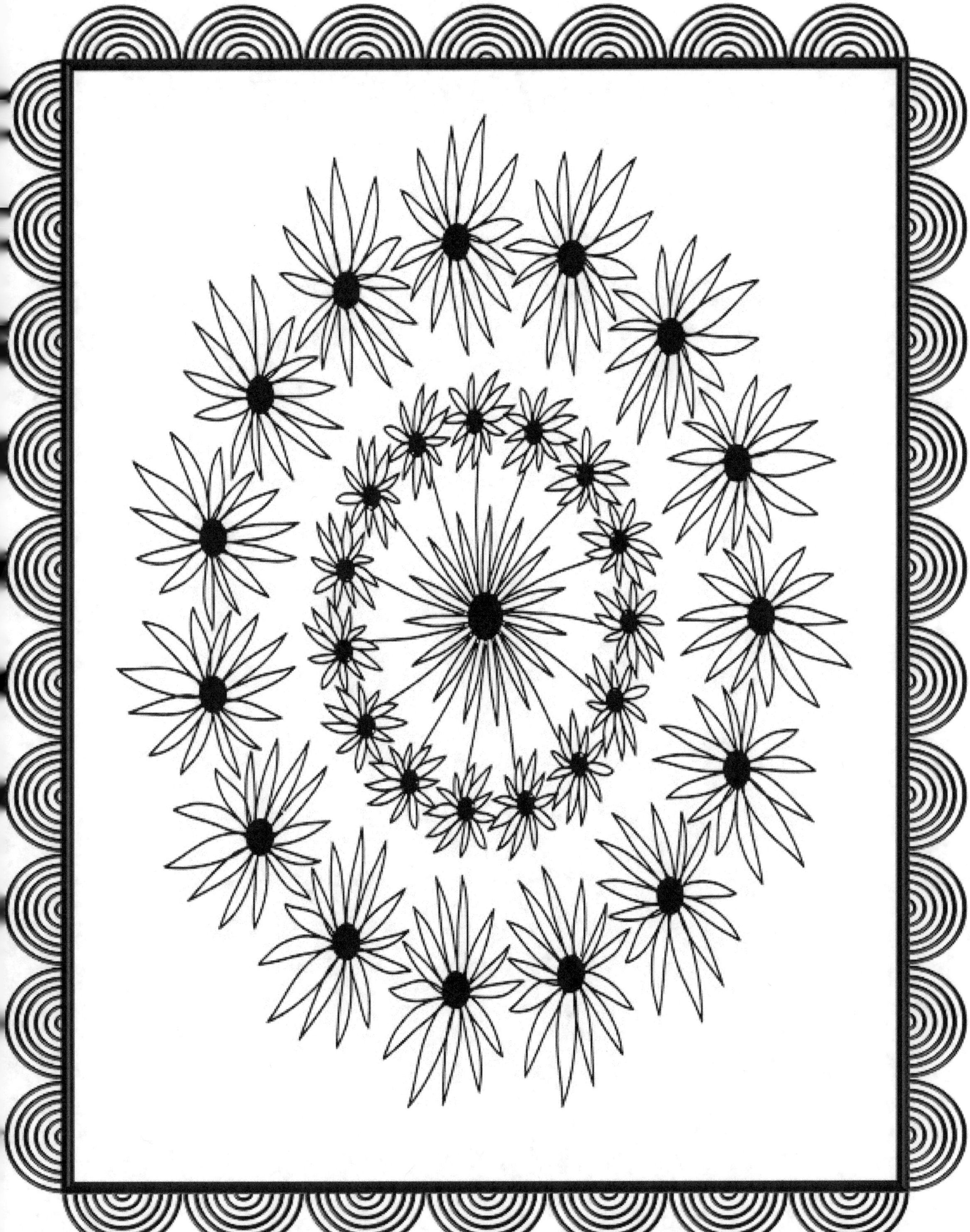

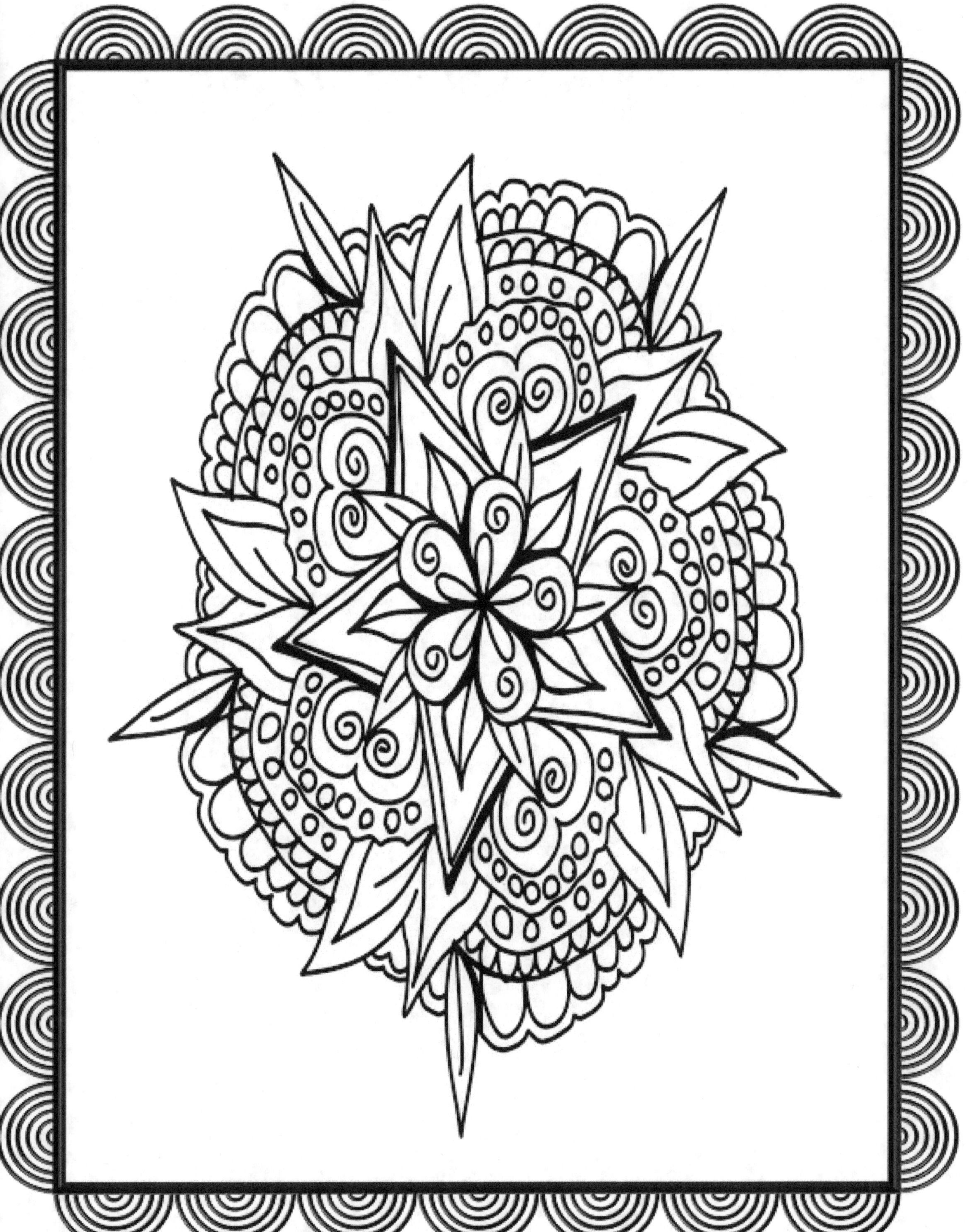

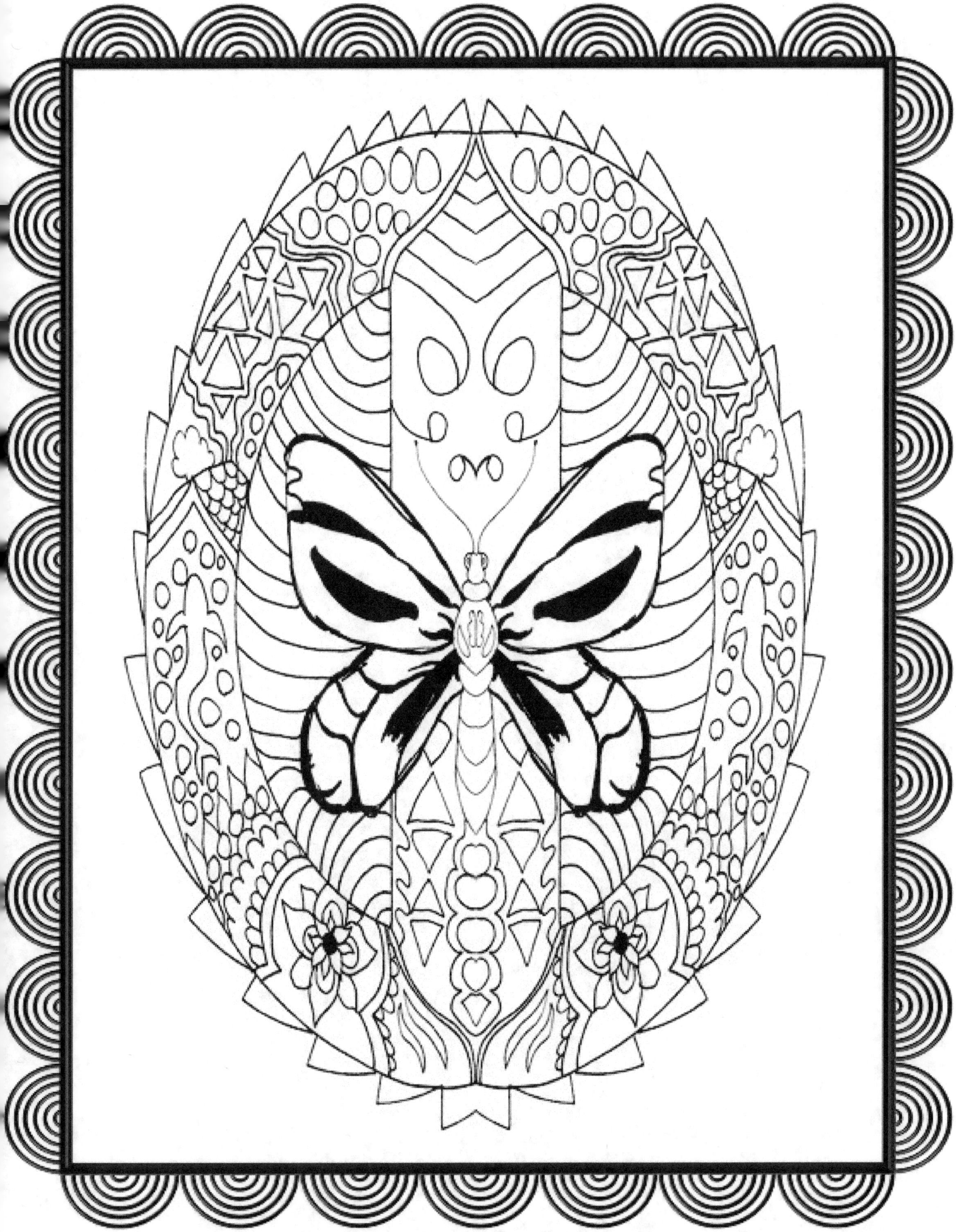

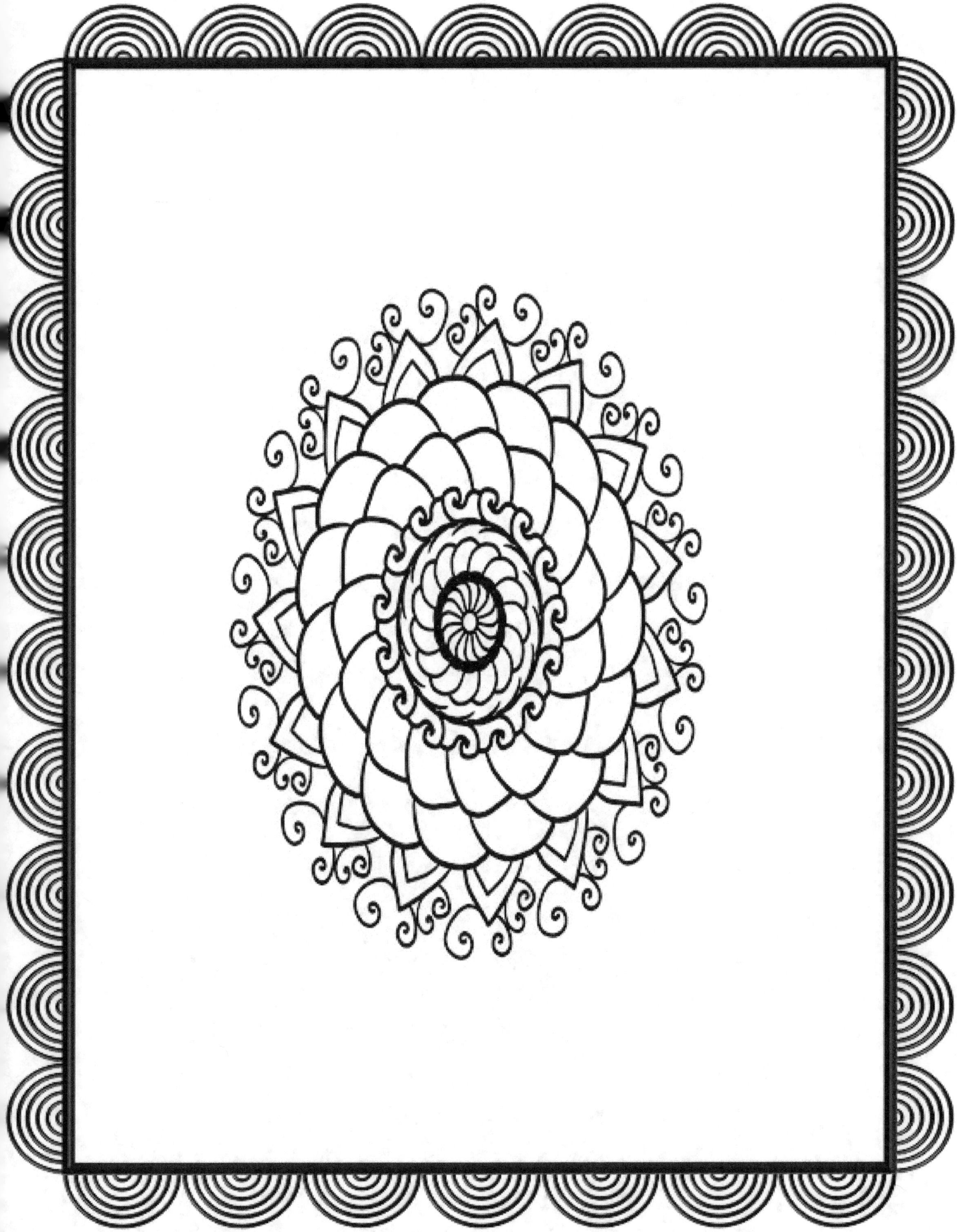

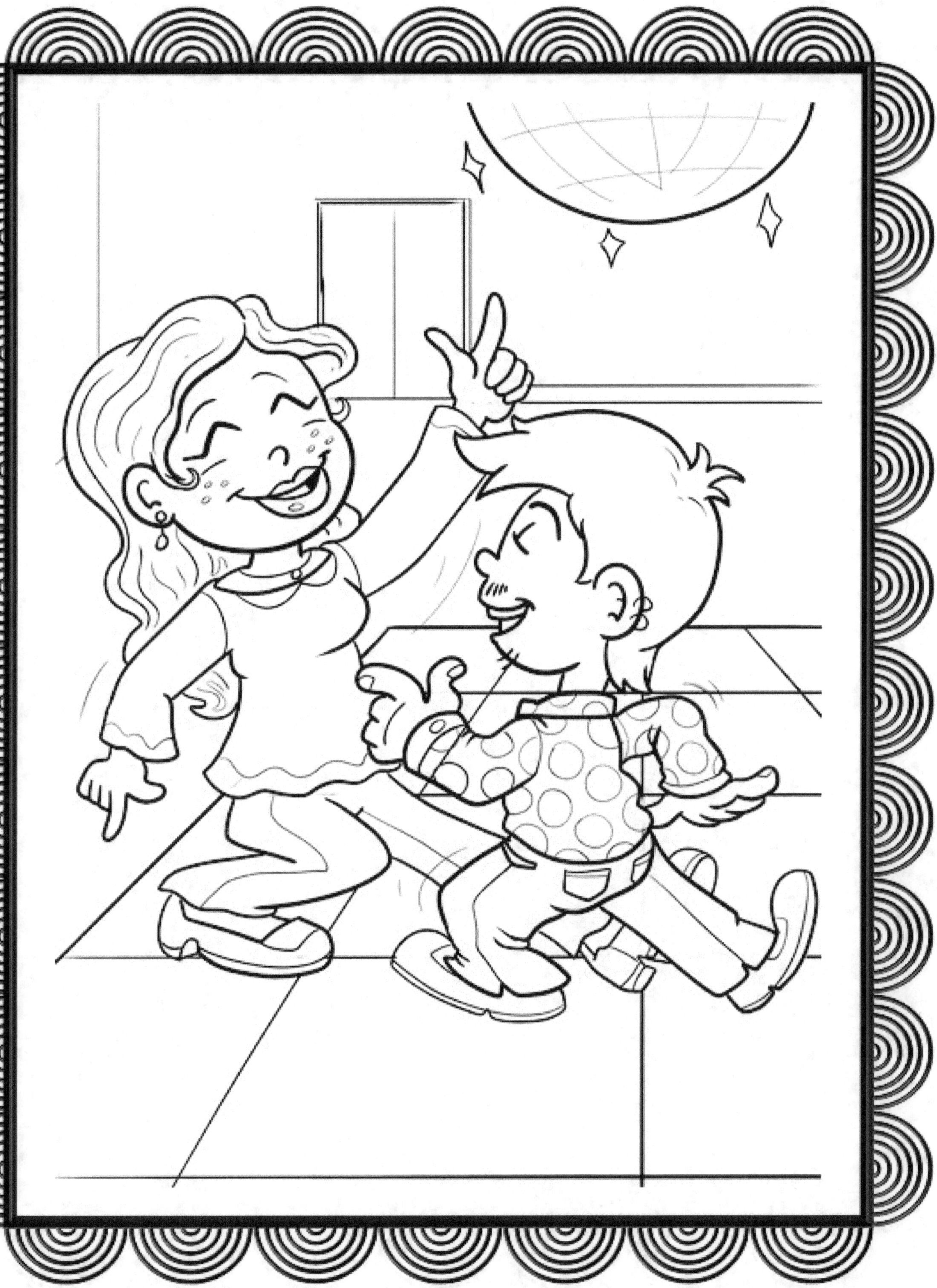

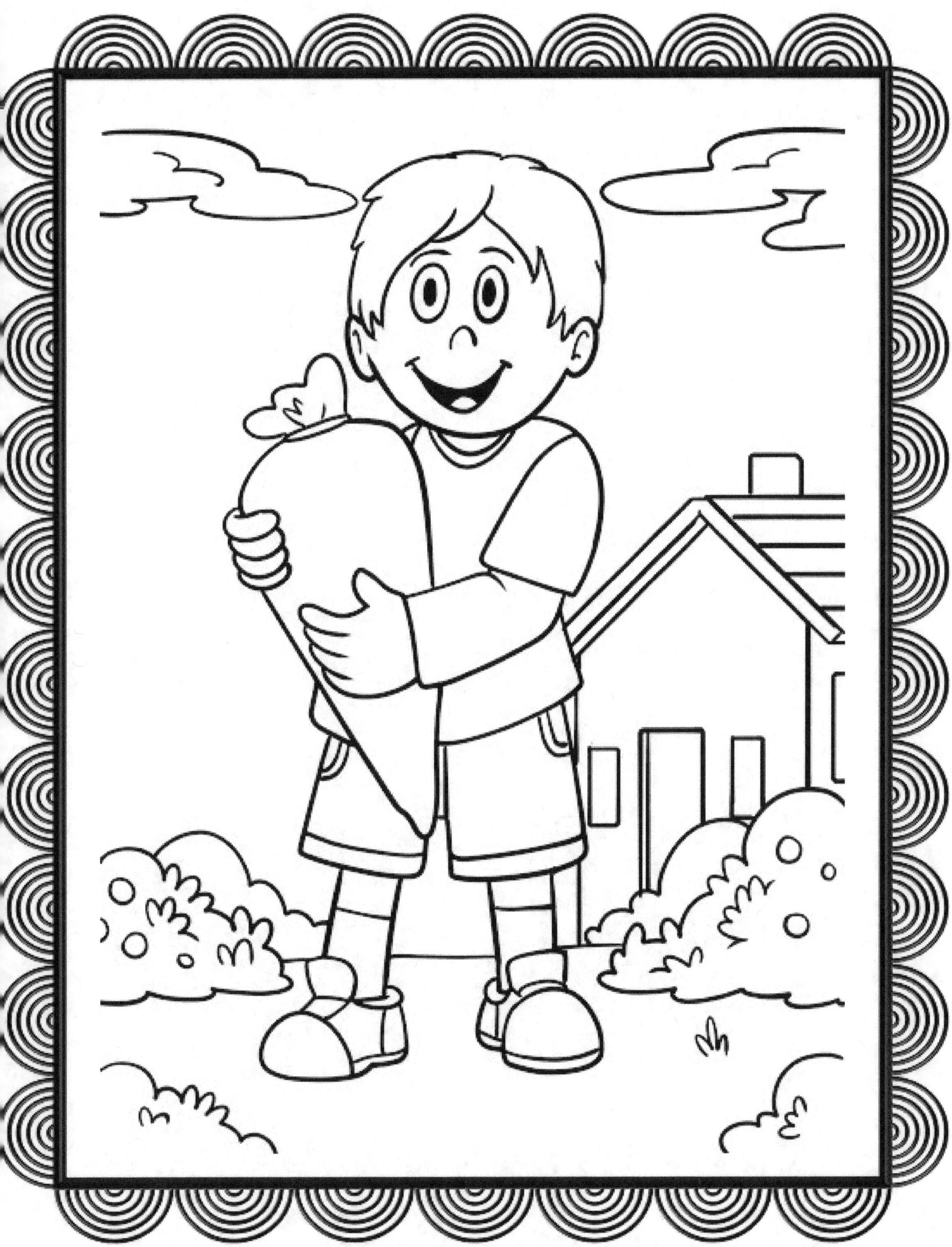

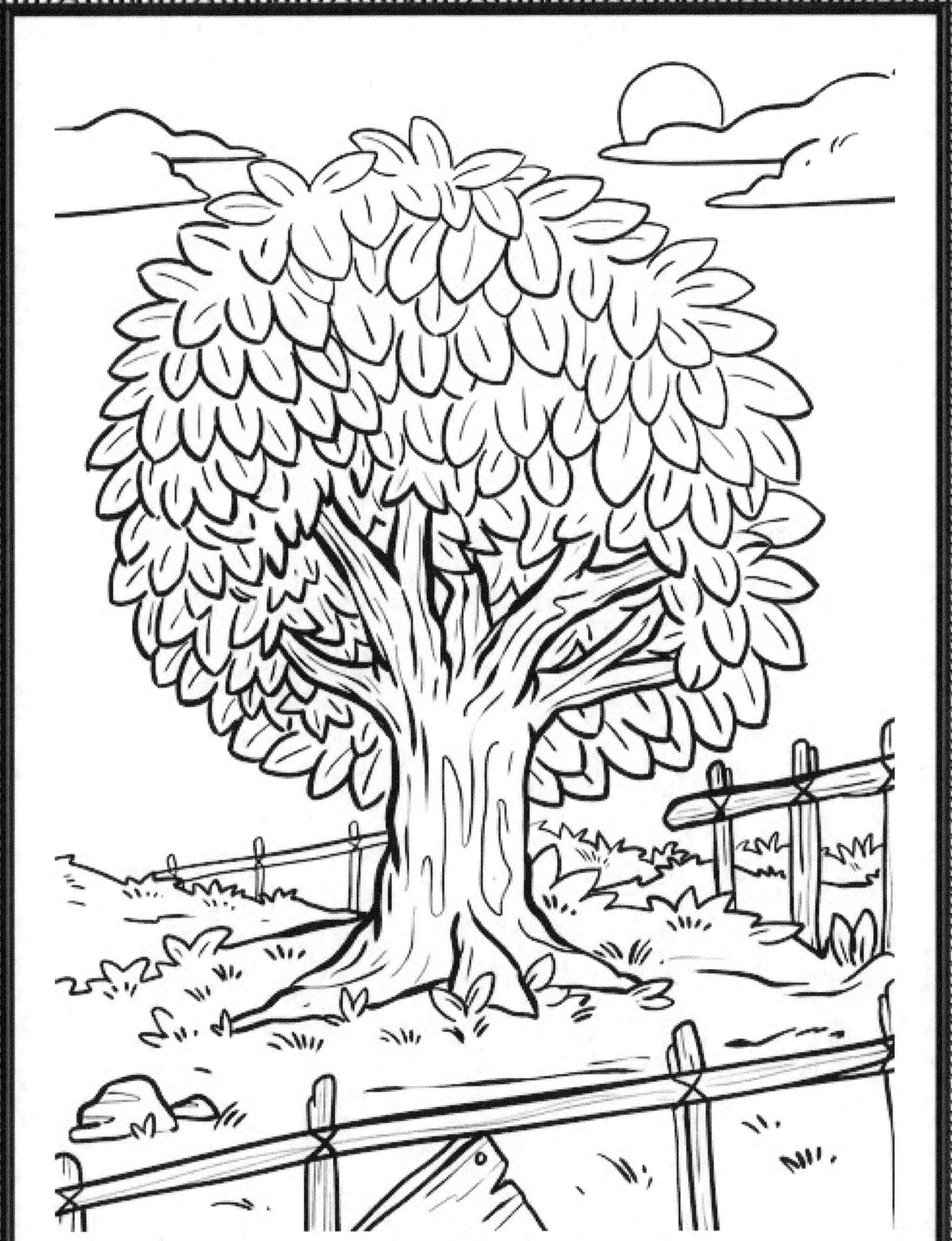

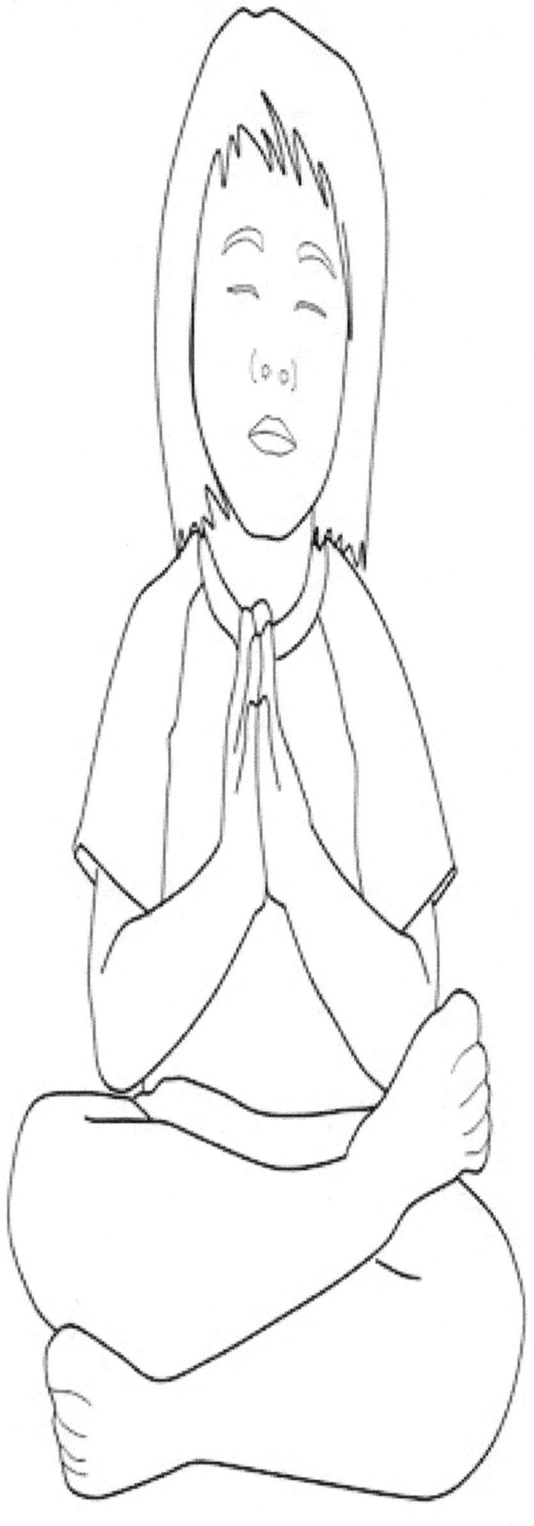

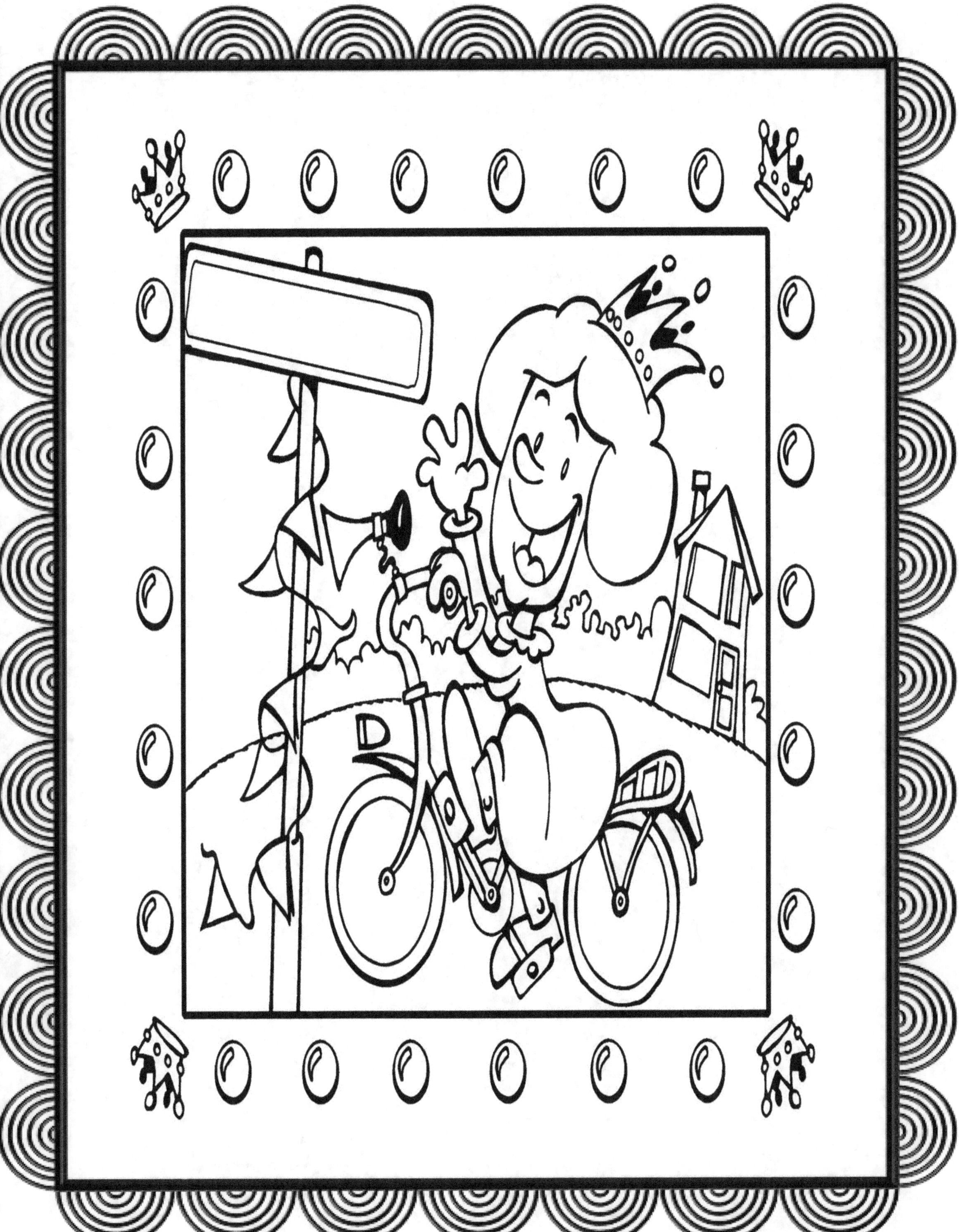

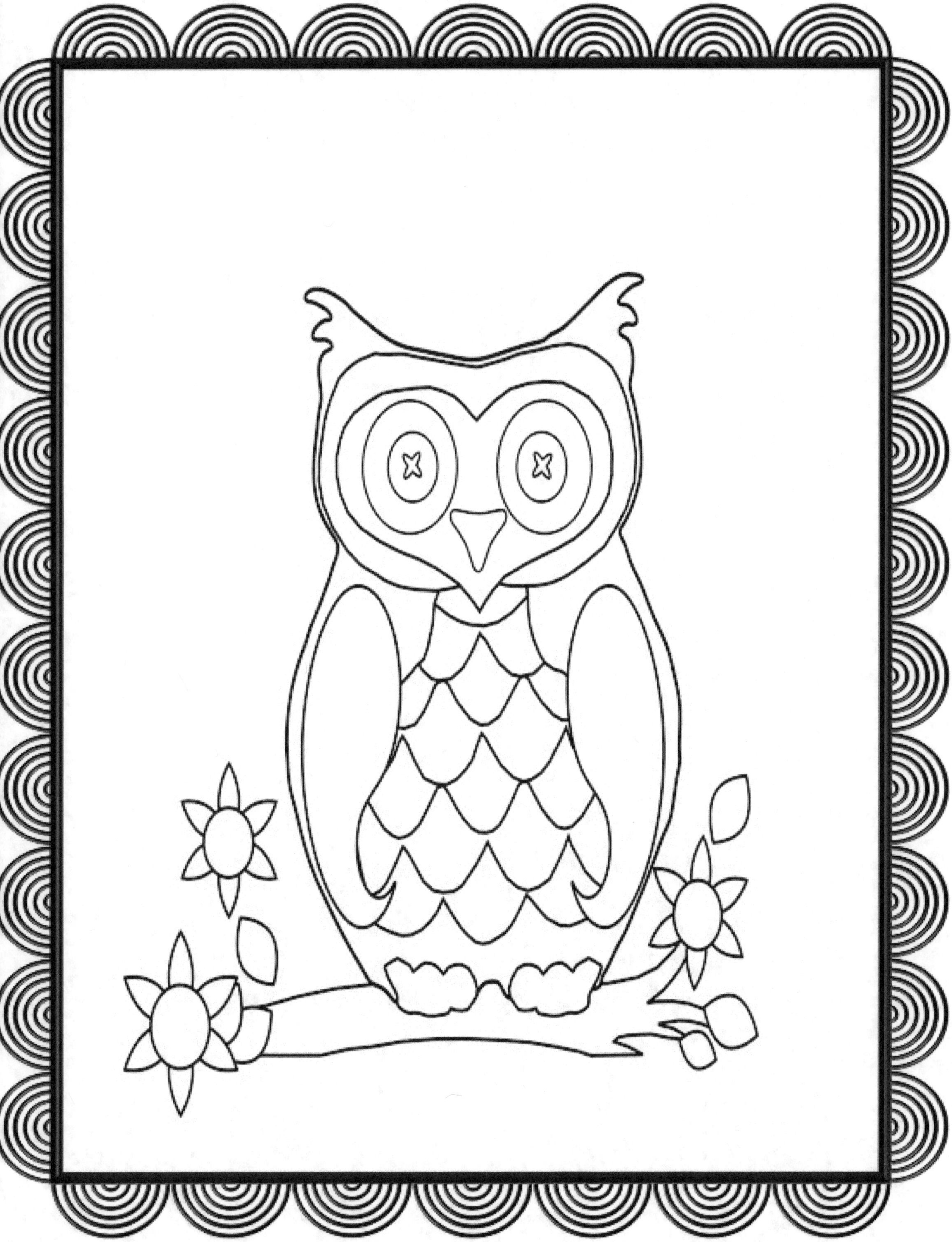

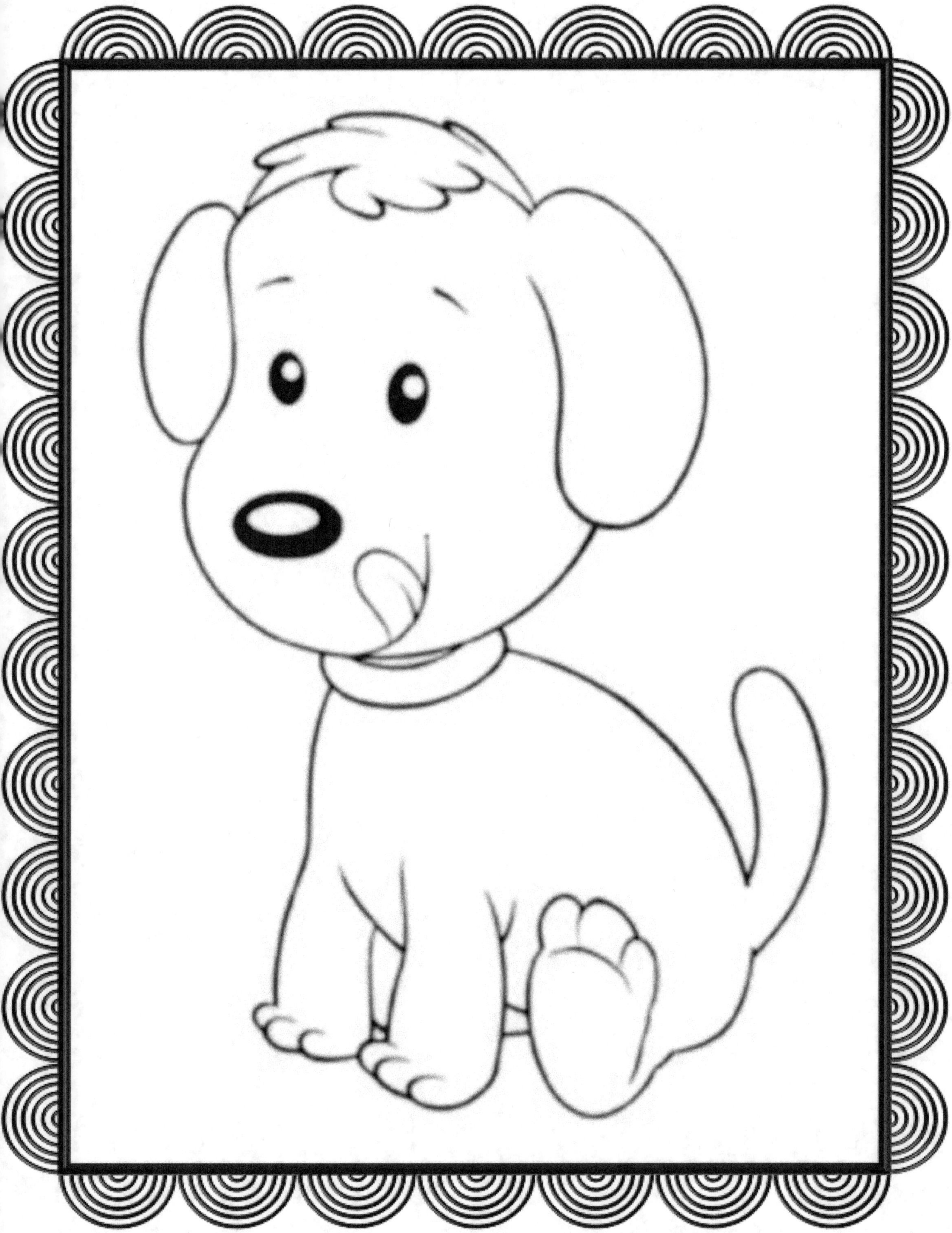

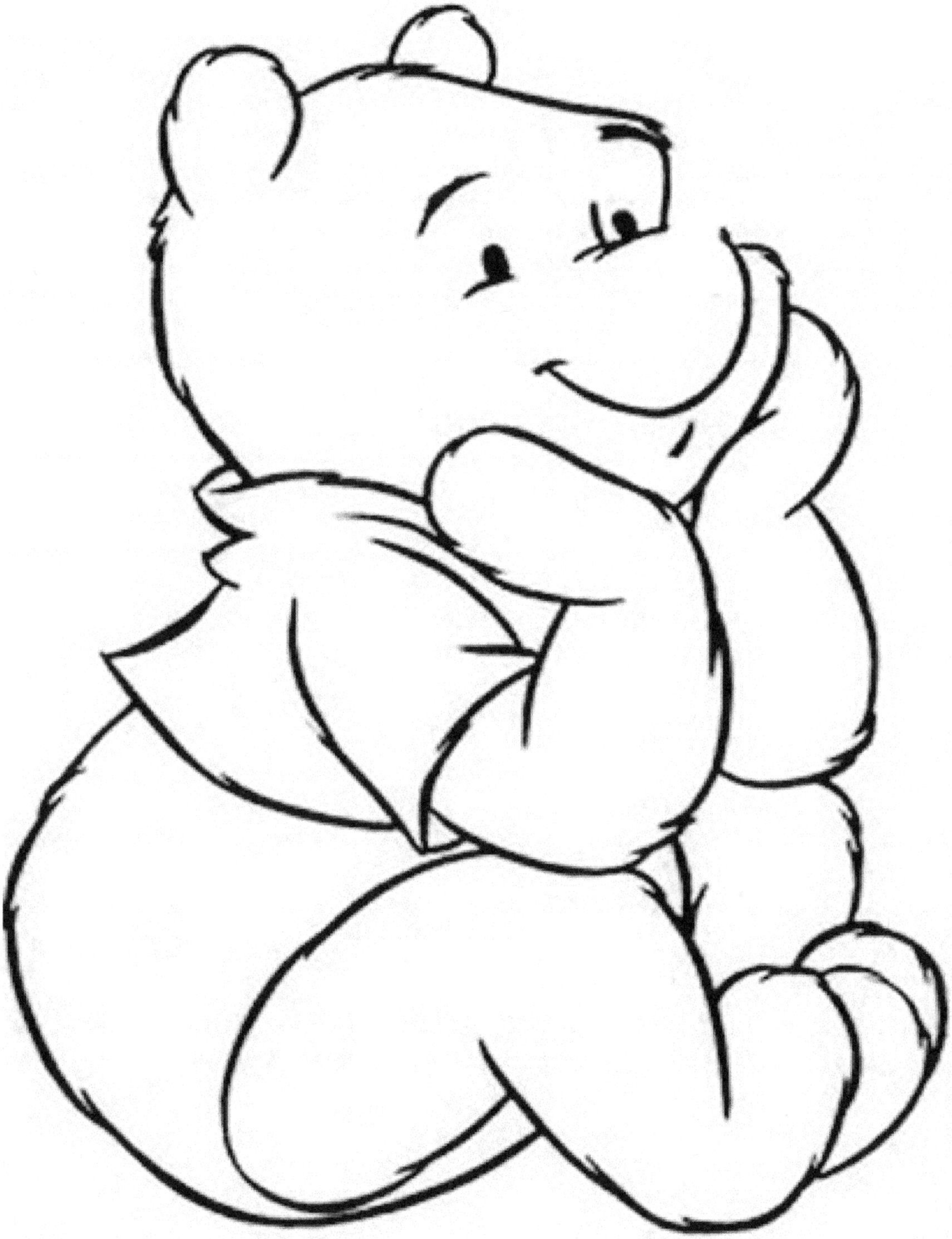

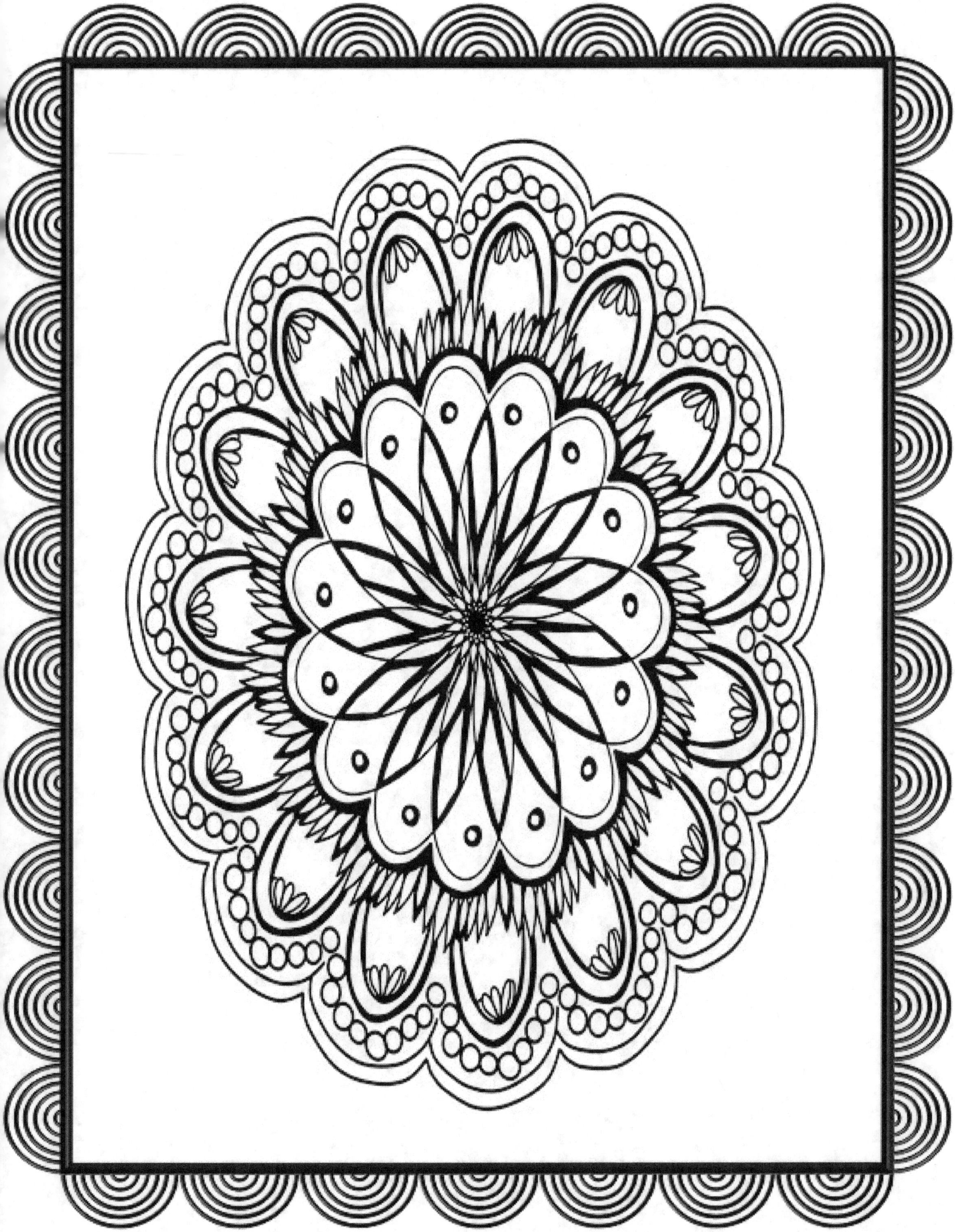

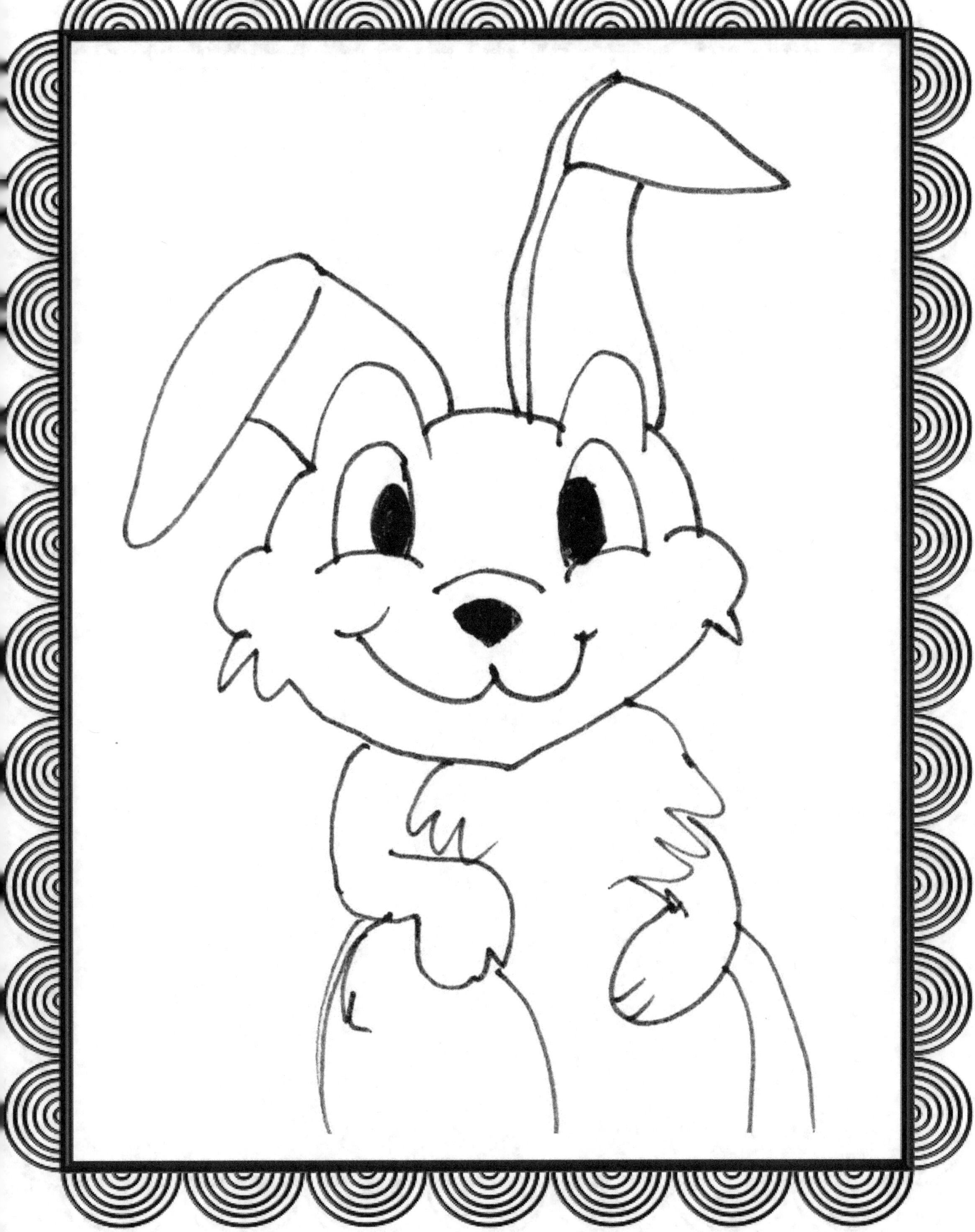

www.ingramcontent.com/pod-product-compliance
Lightning Source LLC
Chambersburg PA
CBHW080955220526
45465CB00008BA/3296